Robert Schumann

~

Scenes from Childhood, Op. 15 (Kinderszenen) - Schumann

Glückes genug.

Wichtige Begebenheit.

No 6.

Träumerei.

No 7.

Am Camin.

Ritter vom Steckenpferd.

Fast zu ernst.

Bonus Music!

Edvard Grieg

~

Grieg: Peer Gynt Suite No. 1 Arr. For Solo Piano

EINFÜHRUNG IN IBSENS „PEER GYNT."
APERÇU DE «PEER GYNT», POÈME DRAMATIQUE DE IBSEN.
FOREWORD TO HENRIK IBSEN'S "PEER GYNT."

Henrik Ibsens, des großen nordischen Geistersehers dramatische Gedichte „Brand" und „Peer Gynt" sind die Höhepunkte einer norwegischen Romantik im 19. Jahrhundert, die wie alle Romantik zu den tiefsten Quellen und Wunden des eigenen Volkstums und Volkscharakters, der eigenen Volkssagen und Märchen hinabsteigt. Man hat in der Gestalt Peer Gynts eine Verkörperung des norwegischen Volkstums und Volkscharakters in einem teilweise stark satirisch angelaufenen Spiegel der eigenen und der fremden Nationen gesehen. Wohl mit Recht. Allein, wie Faust, Don Quichote, Eulenspiegel, Don Juan und Hamlet, ist auch das Einzelpersönliche Peer Gynts ins Allgemein-Menschliche gesteigert. Das Problem des Einzelpersönlichen, das seine Handlungen und Lebensschicksale bestimmt und ihn in unaufhörliche Konflikte mit sich selbst und der äußeren Welt bringt, heißt: wohin führt uns ein Übermaß von Phantasie und ungebändigtem Selbstbewußtsein, wenn jene sich nicht schöpferisch-künstlerisch zu entladen vermag, dieses ein stolzes Freiheits- und Kraftgefühl zu Widerspruch und Übertreibung überspannt?

Wir sehen es an der dreiteiligen äußeren Handlung der Dichtung. Den durch eine phantastisch-haltlose Mutter und einen trunksüchtig-verschwenderischen Vater erblich belasteten Jüngling Peer Gynt treibt beides zu selbstgeglaubten Lügen, zu Rauflust, Trunk und Brautraub (Griegs Peer-Gynt-Suite II, 1) der reichen Ingrid vom Hägstadhof. Schon die nächste Morgenstimmung (Suite I, 1) bringt ihm Reue und Erkenntnis seiner einzigen echten Liebe: Solvejg. Den von der Sippe der verstoßenen Ingrid Geächteten treibt gewolltes Vergessen zu niederster Sinnlichkeit. Phantasie wird abermals Wirklichkeit und führt ihn im Königstraum in die Arme dreier liebestoller Sennerinnen und in die Halle des Bergkönigs (Suite I, 4), des „Dovre-Alten", seines dämonisch-gespenstischen Hofstaates und der ihm zur Ehe versprochenen Trollprinzessin. Als er aber damit selbst Troll und Tier werden soll, erwacht die Erkenntnis seines besseren Selbst und damit sein Gewissen, das zwar immer noch aus Scheu vor nüchterner Wahrheit und tapferer Entscheidung lieber die gewundenen Wege des „Großen Krummen" (allegorische Person) geht, das aber nun auch reine Natur und reine Liebe (Solvejg) schärfen und von unreinen Koboldsgedanken befreien wollen. Zu spät: Gedankensünde — in der häßlichen Dovreprinzessin und ihrem, „seinem" tierischen Sohn verkörpert — treibt ihn von der Geliebten an das Sterbelager seiner alten Mutter — Åses Tod (Suite I, 2) —, der er mit bunten Lügenmärchen das Sterben erleichtert, und danach in die weite Welt.

Avec les poèmes dramatiques «Brand» et «Peer Gynt» du grand visionnaire du nord, Henrik Ibsen, le romantisme norvégien au 19ᵉ siècle atteint à son apogée, et, comme tout romantisme, il puise dans les sources les plus profondes, dans les plaies secrètes de la race, du caractère national, qui ont donné naissance aux légendes et aux contes indigènes.

On a vu se réfléter en Peer Gynt la race, le caractère norvégiens, comme dans un miroir couvert, en partie, d'une assez forte couche de la rosée satirique de son propre peuple autant que des nations étrangères. Cela évidemment avec raison. Cependant, comme l'individualité de Faust, de Don Quichote, d'Eulenspiegel, de Don Juan et de Hamlet, ainsi celle de Peer Gynt a pris des traits qui caractérisent l'humanité entière. Le problème pour l'individu, problème qui va dominer ses actions et décider de son destin, qui le met sans cesse en conflit avec lui-même et le monde extérieur, le voici: où nous mène l'excès d'immagination, la présomption indomptée, si celle-ci ne se métamorphose pas en force créatrice et celle-là, justifiée tant que fière conscience du moi libre et puissant, se livre à la contradiction et à l'exagération.

Nous le voyons par l'action extérieure du poème partagée en trois. L'héritage funeste d'une mère fantastique et sans consistance, d'un père prodigueux, adonné à la boisson, pousse le jeune Peer Gynt au mensonge auquel il croit lui-même, à l'humeur querelleuse, à l'ivrognerie et ——— à enlever la riche fiancée, Ingrid du Hägstadhof (Grieg, Peer Gynt-Suite II, 1). Dès le lendemain de la fuite (Le matin, Suite I, 1) le saisit le repentir et la conscience de son unique amour: Solvejg. Proscrit par la parenté d'Ingrid déshéritée elle-même, l'oubli voulu le livre à la plus basse sensualité. Vision redevient réalité, le mène, dans le rêve du roi, aux pieds de trois vachères amoureuses et dans la halle du roi de montagne (Suite I, 4), devant le «Vieux du Dovre» entouré d'une suite de fantômes diaboliques, et devant la princesse des lutins que l'on veut lui donner en mariage. Avant que l'union puisse se faire, il doit consentir à devenir leur semblable, lutin et brute. C'est là où il reprend conscience de son meilleur moi, là où naissent les scrupules; ils ne sont pas encore de sorte à lui faire vaincre toute peur de la vérité, à lui inspirer le courage prompt à se décider, non, ils le laissent encore suivre les voies tortueuses du «Grand Tortu» (personnage allégorique), tandis que la nature pure et l'amour pur (Solveijg) veulent les aiguiser, veulent le délivrer des idées impures que le contact avec les lutins lui a laissées. Trop tard: le péché de la pensée (incarné en la personne de la laide princesse du Dovre et son fils brutal qui est son

In his dramatic poems, "Brand" and "Peer Gynt", the great Northern visionary, Henrik Ibsen, attains to the height of Norwegian romanticism of the 19ᵗʰ century; which, like all romanticism, draws its subjects from the deepest sources, from the wounds, the sorrows nursed in secret by the nation, stamping its character and giving birth to its traditions and legends. The character of Peer Gynt has been conceived as the incarnation of Norwegian character and spirit, seen as in a mirror reflecting its own people and other nations; only in parts strong tarnished or dulled with the breath of satire. And, perhaps, rightly so. Yet, not unlike the individuality of a Faust, a Don Quixote, a Till Eulenspiegel, a Don Juan or a Hamlet, that of Peer Gynt has assumed traits characteristic of humanity at large. As to the problem attending individuality, dominating its actions, determining its destiny and involving it in constant conflict with itself and the outer world, the question arises: what is to be the outcome of excessive fancy allowed to roam at large, of unbridled presumption and self-conceit, if the one cannot unburden itself in creative art, the other, justified in its proud consciousness of freedom, power and strength, fall a victim to contradiction and exaggeration.

This is shown clearly in the setting of the drama, the argument, being divided into three parts. The fatal heirdom of a fanatic-infirm mother, of a drunkard-spendthrift father drives the youth, Peer Gynt, the scion of such wretched parents, on to deception and falsehood, in which he eventually believes himself even; he develops a quarrelsome spirit, takes to drinking, and is finally misled to carry off a girl he is betrothed to, —Rape of the Betrothed—(Grieg's PeerGynt-Suite II, 1), the rich Ingrid on Hägstadhof. But even the next Dawn-of-Morning (Suite I, 1) brings repentance, and consciousness of his only true love: Solvejg. Proscribed by the kinsmen of Ingrid, herself cast out, self-enforced oblivion spurs him on to the lowest degree of sensuality. Once more, imagination becomes reality, and, in his "King-Dream", leads him into the arms of three love-mad dairy-maids and into the hall of the King of the Mountains (Suite I, 4), into the presence of the "Old Man of Dovre" surrounded by his demons and ghostly phantoms, and of the troll princess whom he is to marry. But as this union would metamorphise him into a troll and wild beast, he awakens to the consciousness of his better self; his conscience is roused, which, however, still shrinking from facing the naked truth, and lacking the moral courage to form a definite decision, prefers to continue wandering in the crooked paths and ways of the "Great Crook", (allegorical person). Pure nature and pure love (Solvejg) are, however, at work pricking his conscience and striving to free it from impure thought which its contact with the hobgoblins has implanted, and left, in it. Too late! Sin in Thought — embodied in the ugly Dovre Princess and her, "his", bestial son, — drives him forth from the beloved one to the death-bed of his aged mother, whose last

Der Mann Peer Gynt lebt ein zügelloses Abenteurerleben. Die Menschen sind ihm als Repräsentanten der heimlich von ihm verspotteten Nationen lediglich Sachen zu Gelderwerb und Reichtum geworden, der liebe Gott ist sein umschmeichelter, ganz besonderer väterlicher Schützer. Ein Projekt folgt dem anderen. Im Traum eines Kaisertums der Wüste gefällt er sich in der Rolle eines von schönen Arabermädchen — Anitras Tanz (Suite I, 3) und Arabischer Tanz (Suite II, 3) — verehrten Propheten. Der Traum ist dank Anitras Mutterwitz bald aus, nur ein blasses, rasch verlöschendes Traumgesicht (Solvejg) bleibt von ihm übrig. Die Musik der Memnonssäule, die Rätsel der Sphinx in Ägypten sagen ihm, der nun ein dilettierender Altertumsforscher ward, nichts. Erst das Irrenhaus in Kairo mit seinen entsetzlichen Szenen geben ihm des Rätsels Lösung: Sich selbst als krasser Egoist und Realist genug sein ohne Ziel und Verantwortung ist mit Irrsinn gleichbedeutend.

Der Greis Peer Gynt, ein anderer Ahasver und Fliegender Holländer, erleidet in gewaltigem Sturm angesichts der norwegischen Küste — Peer Gynts Heimkehr (Suite II, 3) — Schiffbruch, rettet sich, kommt gerade recht zur Versteigerung seines letzten Erbteiles, hört unerkannt das vernichtende Urteil des Volkes über sich selbst und lebt nun sein ganzes verfehltes und verlorenes Leben noch einmal, allein auf wilder Heide. Die Handlung wird ganz Allegorie und Symbol. Der unheimliche „Knopfgießer", der ihn umschmelzen will, der zum alten Bettler heruntergekommene Dovre-Alte, der „Magere" — sie alle sind nur die verkörperten Stimmen seines eigenen aufgewühlten Gewissens, das ihm sagt: du warst dir selbst in allen Lagen des Lebens genug, allein du warst, unbekannt mit dem wahren Sinn des Lebens, niemals du selbst! Nur ein besseres Ich ruht tief unter den Trümmern der Bergeslast seines Lebens: Solvejg, die reine Geliebte, die in geduldigem Warten auf den Geliebten alt, grau und blind geworden ist. In ihren Schoß als in den der alles erkennenden und alles verzeihenden Mutter gebettet, wird Peer Gynt mit Solvejgs Wiegenlied zur ewigen Ruhe gesungen. Des Rätsels Lösung ist gefunden: Glaube, Liebe, Hoffnung.

Wenn diese tiefsinnige und ganz und gar im norwegischen Volk und Boden wurzelnde Gedankendichtung außerhalb ihrer Heimat dauernde Verbreitung und neues Leben auf der Bühne gewann, so verdankt sie das nicht zum geringen Teile Edvard Griegs herrlicher Musik (1874—76*). Ja, sie ist es doch wohl in erster Linie gewesen, die als vielleicht kostbarste Blüte der norwegischen musikalischen Romantik die dichterische in Ibsens „Peer Gynt" weiteren Kreisen erst erschlossen und verständlich gemacht hat.

Walter Niemann

fils à lui aussi) le fait fuir l'aimée pour se jeter aux genoux de sa vielle mère mourante — mort d'Åses (Suite I, 3) dont il apaise l'angoisse par de petites historiettes — controuvées. Alors l'attire le monde, il s'y jette, à corps et âme perdus...

Peer Gynt homme vit la vie débauchée d'un aventurier. Les hommes, représentant les nations dont il se moque en secret ne sont pour lui que des choses dont on se sert pour tirer profit, pour arriver à la fortune, et le bon Dieu, c'est un patron paternel à lui qu'il faut flatter. Un projet suit l'autre. Immaginant un empire aux déserts, il se plaît dans le rôle d'un prophète vénéré de jolies filles arabes. — Danse d'Anitra (Suite I, 3.) — et — Danse arabe (Suite II, 3.) — Grâce au bon sens d'Anitra, cette chimère va bientôt finir et rien n'y survit qu'une vision frêle (Solvejg) qui, elle aussi, va s'éteindre. Quoique devenu archéologue par goût, la musique de la colonne de Memnon, les énigmes de la sphinx d'Egypte ne lui disent rien. Ce ne sont que les scènes horribles qu'il voit dans l'hospice des aliénés au Caire qui lui dévoilent le problème de la vie: être le pire des égoistes, réaliste impassible, n'avoir ni but ni responsabilité dans la vie et en être content, tout à fait content, voilà ce qui touche à l'égarement d'esprit.

Peer Gynt vieillard, second Ahasvérus, autre Hollandais au Vaisseau Fantôme fait naufrage par une effroyable tempête en vue de son pays natal (Repatriement de Peer Gynt) (Suite II, 3), se sauve, vient justement à temps pour voir aux enchères le dernier brin de son héritage, apprend, sans être connu, combien est sévère le jugement que lui rendent ses concitoyens et revit sa vie perdue enfoncé dans la solitude. L'action devient entièrement allégorique et symbolique. Le sinistre fondeur de boutons qui le veut refondre, le vieux du Dovre, tombé au plus bas et mendiant, le «Maigre», ce ne sont tous que les remords de sa conscience remuée sous forme corporelle qui lui disent: quelle que fut la situation, tu as toujours fait ce que tu as voulu, le sens de la vie, pourtant, tu ne l'as pas compris et jamais tu n'as été toi-même. Les débris de sa vie ne couvrent qu'un seul nom digne de souvenir: Solvejg, l'amante pure, vieillie dans l'attente de l'aimée, aux cheveux blanchis, aux yeux eteints. Sur son cœur, le cœur de la mère qui comprend tout et pardonne tout, il s'endort du dernier sommeil aux sons de sa voix. Telle est la solution du problème: la foi, l'espérance, l'amour.

Si ce poème profond dont la racine est entièrement dans le sol norvégien a trouvé bon accueil et ce qui est plus, succès solide sur la scène en dehors du pays natal, il le doit, non pas pour le moins, à la musique merveilleuse d'Edvard Grieg (1874—76*). Elle, peut-être le fruit le plus précieux du romantisme musical norvégien a frayé la voie à la gloire du Peer Gynt de Henrik Ibsen en le mettant à la portée de beaucoup.

moments he alleviates by telling her all sorts of self-invented fairy-tales, and then, off he sets into the wide wild world.

The man Peer Gynt lives the loose life of an adventurer. His fellow-men, the representatives of the nations he secretly derides and makes fun of, are become to him milk-cows, merely objects from which to derive profit and wealth; the Lord of Heaven flattered by him in words, being his own special Protector. One scheme follows the other in rapid succession. In his dreams of founding an empire of the desert, he delights in his rôle as a prophet worshipped by beautiful Arab maidens — Anitra's Dance — (Suite I, 3) and — Arabian Dance (Suite II, 3). — But the good common sense of Anitra soon puts an end to this dream, and nothing survives of it but a pale stet phantom (Solvejg), fast fading into naught. The music of the Memnon statue, the riddles of the Sphinx in Egypt disclose nothing to him, who has in the meantime turned amateur antiquarian. And nothing short of the horrible scenes he witnesses in the lunatic-Asylum at Cairo affords him a solution of life's problem: To find self-sufficiency in coarse egotism and realism, to live on without an object, or feeling of responsibility in life, is equivalent to insanity.

Peer Gynt, now an aged man, a second Ahasverus, or Flying Dutchman, is wrecked in a terrific storm just off the coast of Norway — Peer Gynt's Return home (Suite II, 3); he manages to save himself, and arrives home just in time to witness the sale by auction of his last inheritance, and to hear, incognito, the crushing judgment pronounced upon him by his fellow-citizens, by the people. He retires to the solitude of the wild moorlands, and there lives his wasted life over again. The scene now becomes allegorical and symbolical throughout. The uncanny "button-founder", who wants to new-mould him, the "Ancient One of Dovre" now reduced to beggary, the "Emaciated One" — are all of them but the incarnate voices of his troubled conscience roused into action, and calling him to account, reminding him: "In all states and conditions of life, thou wert ever satisfied with thine own self alone, and yet, ignorant of the true meaning of life, thou wert never thine own self!" The ruins from the wreck of his wretched life cover but one better ego, one name worthy of remembrance: Solvejg, the purely beloved one, who has grown old, grey and blind, waiting for the coming of him she loves. Bedded in her lap, as in that of a mother who understands, and forgives, all, Peer Gynt is sung to eternal rest, soothed by the lilt of Solvejg's Lullaby. Thus the solution of the problem reads: Faith, Hope and Charity.

The fact of this mysterious poem, with its thread of deep thoughts rooted in Norwegian soil, having met with such a hearty welcome and success on the theatre-stages of foreign countries far from its native home, is due, in no small degree, to Edvard Grieg's glorious music (1874—76*). It may even be said, that it was, probably, this very music, the most precious blossom of Norwegian musical romanticism, which opened out, and interpreted, to wider circles the poetical romance and beauty in Ibsen's Peer Gynt.

---

*) Vergl. Gerhard Schjelderup-Walter Niemann, Edvard Grieg. Biographie und Würdigung seiner Werke. Leipzig, C. F. Peters, S. 139 ff.

*) Comparez Gerhard Schjelderup-Walter Niemann, Edvard Grieg, «Biographie et appréciation de ses œuvres». Leipzig. C. F. Peters, pag. 139 ff.

*) cf. Gerhard Schelderup - Walter Niemann, Edvard Grieg. Biography and Estimation of his Works. Leipzig. C. F. Peters Page 139 et seq.

INHALT
CONTENU – CONTENTS

No. 1. MORGENSTIMMUNG 5
LE MATIN. MORNING-MOOD.

No. 2. ÅSES TOD 10
LA MORT D'ÅSE. THE DEATH OF ÅSE.

No. 3. ANITRAS TANZ 12
LA DANSE D'ANITRA. ANITRA'S DANCE.

No. 4. IN DER HALLE DES BERG-KÖNIGS 16
DANS LA HALLE DU ROI DE MONTAGNE.
IN THE HALL OF THE MOUNTAIN-KING.

I
Morgenstimmung
Le matin — Morning-mood

Edvard Grieg, Op. 46

II
Åses Tod
La mort d'Åse — The death of Åse

III
Anitras Tanz
La danse d'Anitra — Anitra's dance

*) Die Triller ohne Nachschlag.

IV
In der Halle des Bergkönigs
Dans la halle du roi de montagne — In the hall of the mountain-king

Alla marcia e molto marcato M.M. ♩ = 138

17

Made in the USA
Monee, IL
04 July 2022